THE BATTLE OF GETTYSBURG

The Turning Point of the American Civil War

Written by Michaël Antoine
In collaboration with Thomas Jacquemin
Translated by Carly Probert

History 50MINUTES.com

THE BATTLE OF GETTYSBURG

KEY INFORMATION

- **When:** 1-3 July 1863
- **Where:** South of Gettysburg (Pennsylvania, USA)
- **Context:** The American Civil War (1861-1865)
- **Belligerents:** The Union (north of the present-day United States) against the Confederate States of the south of the present-day United States
- **Commanders and leaders:**
  - Robert Edward Lee, commanding general of the Confederate troops (1807-1870)
  - George Edward Pickett, Confederate general (1825-1875)
  - George Gordon Meade, commanding general of the Army of the Potomac of the Union (1815-1872)
- **Outcome:** Union victory
- **Victims:**
  - Unionist camp: approximately 3 000 dead, 15 000 wounded and 5 000 captured
  - Confederate camp: approximately 5 000 dead, 13 000 wounded and 6 000 captured

INTRODUCTION

The Battle of Gettysburg was fought between the troops of the Union and the Confederate troops during the American Civil War. Won by the northern troops, the ground combat is often considered one of the turning points of the war and one of the bloodiest of the conflict. On both sides, losses were particularly high.

The American nation, which was still relatively new, was in a deep crisis in the 1860s that saw many states pitted against one another over the topic of slavery: the states located in the north wanted to abolish slavery, while those in the south opposed this fiercely, fearing for their economy which was based on an agrarian society, where the exploitation of slaves was paramount. This quarrel gave rise to two clans: the Union, which included the northern states, and the Confederacy, which consisted of 11 states that decided to secede.

From the beginning of the war until the middle of 1863, the armies of Confederate General Robert Edward Lee dominated the Unionist troops, without winning a decisive battle. Seeking to strike a fatal blow to the opponent, he advanced his armies into Union territory. The northern troops, determined to prevent a threat to Washington, accidentally came across the Confederate Army at Gettysburg on 1st July 1863. This was followed by three days of battle, in which the southern troops tried in vain to pierce the defenses of the northern armies, which held on with difficulty. On 3 July 1863, realizing that the fighting was in vain and particularly bloody, General Robert Edward Lee decided to retreat, thus accepting defeat.

POLITICAL AND SOCIAL CONTEXT

THE ABOLITION OF SLAVERY AND THE SECESSION

The Civil War saw the U.S. divide over the question of slavery. From the 1850s, the gap between the northern states, which were abolitionists, and the southern states, which were pro-slavery, became unbridgeable. While in the north, the abolition of slavery was considered necessary for a country that advocated equality and freedom, in the south, states were fundamentally opposed to the idea because their agrarian economy depended on slavery. The workforce was absolutely necessary for their cotton.

Tensions between the north and the south peaked in 1860, when the Republican candidate Abraham Lincoln (1809-1865) became the 16th president of the United States. During the election campaign, not a single southern state gave him support because he presented himself as being deeply opposed to slavery. Refusing to be led by a man whose convictions were contrary to their own, they decided to secede, following the lead of South Carolina, which was the first to do so. From 4 February 1861, the Confederate States of America was created and led by an interim president, Jefferson Davis (1808-1889), who moved to the new capital of Richmond.

Meanwhile, Abraham Lincoln refused the separation imposed by the southern states and considered using force to bring them back within the Union. Both sides had to prepare for a war that seemed inevitable. However, the stakes were different for the two entities that would compete:

- The southern secessionists were not trying to conquer the north; they only wanted to preserve their type of society and economy. Therefore, the implemented strategy involved exhausting the northerners until peace was proclaimed.
- The northern abolitionists wished to prove that they held the truth and that slavery was contrary to the values defended by the United States. To do this, the annihilation of the Confederacy had to be total.

THE BALANCE OF POWER

On both sides, it was believed that the war would be short. Each of them had their strengths to tip the battle in their favor. The southerners were outnumbered – the secessionist states had only 5.45 million inhabitants – and were less industrialized, however they had excellent soldiers and officers. In addition, the Confederates, seen as a new nationality in Europe, aroused sympathy at a time when nationalism reached its peak. Finally, the Confederacy had the final advantage of the cohesion of its territory, which meant it did not have to disperse its forces.

The Unionists were superior in number – 18.95 million people lived within the Union – and had excellent industries, a developed railway system and a strong economy. These advantages also prevented the Europeans from intervening in favor of the southerners. However, Abraham Lincoln and his government found it very difficult to mobilize men and resources for a conflict that seemed far away in the eyes of many. Finally, a definite disadvantage was that the Union did not have troops that were as qualified as its opponent.

THE BEGINNING OF THE WAR

The Civil War began on 12 April 1861. Soon, the Union troops closed the borders of the breakaway states and set up a naval blockade to strangle the economy of the enemy. However, the commander of the Confederates, Robert Edward Lee, who was an excellent tactician, managed to keep the northern troops in check. Yet, each Confederate success was gained at the cost of many casualties. Robert Edward Lee was aware that the Confederates had to quickly gain a clear victory in order to improve the situation in the southern states.

COMMANDERS AND LEADERS

ROBERT EDWARD LEE, COMMANDING GENERAL OF THE CONFEDERATE TROOPS

Portrait of Robert Edward Lee by Julian Vannerson.

Born in Stratford Hall Plantation (Virginia) in 1807, Robert Edward Lee was an American general commanding the Confederate Army during the Civil War. Having graduated from the Military Academy at West Point as an engineer officer, he enlisted in the U.S. Army and participated in the war against Mexico (1846-1848), where he had already distinguished himself through abilities as an officer.

Coming from a wealthy family and the father of seven children, Robert Edward Lee wanted slavery to be abolished. While he was promoted to the rank of general in the federal army and although he was opposed to secession, which he considered to be a betrayal of his country, he refused to take up arms against his own state (Virginia), who had just joined the Confederate camp. When freeing his own slaves in 1861, Robert Edward Lee then enrolled in the southern camp and was appointed commander of the Army of Northern Virginia before becoming a military adviser to President Jefferson Davis. Distinguished by his qualities as a tactician, he was promoted to General of the Army of the Confederate States in 1865. Despite his many successes, he could not prevent the defeat of his camp: thus, he was forced to sign the surrender at Appomattox in Virginia on 9 April 1865.

However, Robert Edward Lee was happy that the war was ending and that slavery was to be abolished. After an oath of allegiance to the United States, the former general became President of Washington College in Lexington from October 1865. In 1870, he died of pneumonia.

GEORGE EDWARD PICKETT, CONFEDERATE GENERAL

Portrait of George Edward Pickett.

Born in Richmond (Virginia) in 1825, George Edward Pickett was a loyal American general to the southern cause during the American Civil War.

Graduating from West Point in 1846, he began his military career during the war between the United States and Mexico. Having obtained his captain's stripes, George Edward Pickett continued his career in various units. Like General Robert Edward Lee, he was opposed to slavery. However, like his commander, when the state of Virginia seceded, he enlisted in the Confederate army. Gaining the ranks of major and colonel in turn, he participated in several battles and was distinguished by his tactical skills. In September 1862, he was given command of a division belonging to the Army Corps of his friend, General James Longstreet (1821-1904).

At the Battle of Gettysburg, George Edward Pickett and his division undertook a terrible and bloody charge on 3 July. Indeed, of the 15 000 men in the employee's division, three quarters were killed or wounded, including three brigadier generals and 13 colonels. George Edward Pickett proved completely desperate, and it was General Robert Edward Lee who would take responsibility for this disaster. Subsequently, he participated in the defense of the Confederate capital, Richmond, and the siege of Petersburg. Finally, taking part in the Battle of Appomattox, he was defeated like the rest of the southern army and fled to Canada where he remained until 1866. Returning to Norfolk, where he attempted to be rehabilitated, George Edward Picket died on 30 July 1875.

GEORGE GORDON MEADE, COMMANDING GENERAL OF THE ARMY OF POTOMAC

Portrait of George Gordon Meade by Matthew Brady.

Born in Cadiz (Spain) in 1815, George Gordon Meade was an American general, loyal the Union during the Civil War. A graduate of the prestigious officers' school of West Point and the son of the consul general of the United States in Spain, he chose to leave the army in 1836 to become a civil engineer. In 1842, he decided to resume service and fought in the ranks of the U.S. military against the Indians and against the Mexicans.

At the beginning of the Civil War, George Gordon Meade was promoted to brigadier general and participated in several battles in the Army of the Potomac (main Union army). Wounded in Glendale, he recovered and took part in further battles. Although he turned out to be a good commander, he had to follow orders from the indecisive General Joseph Hooker (1814-1879), who was responsible for the unexpected defeat at Chancellorsville.

<u>**Good to know**</u>

The Battle of Chancellorsville (27 April-6 May 1863) was an important fight in which the Confederate Army of General Robert Edward Lee routed the troops of General Joseph Hooker. Despite a numerically larger opponent (the ratio was two against one in favour of the northerners), General Robert Edward Lee, being an outstanding tactician, knew how to perfectly exploit the tactical weakness and hesitations of his opponents. This surprise defeat led to the loss of confidence of President Abraham Lincoln in Joseph Hooker, who would resign from his post in June 1863.

In June 1863, President Abraham Lincoln accepted his resignation and replaced him with George Gordon Meade who obeyed reluctantly, not feeling able to lead an army. Yet, he was put in charge of the command of the Union army at the Battle of Gettysburg, during which he managed to cleverly exploit the field to counter the violent attacks ordered by General Robert Edward Lee. Although he eventually won that bloody battle, George Gordon Meade did not dare to pursue the southern army in retreat, for fear of suffering even more casualties. The war was not over and, from 1863 to 1865, he commanded the Army of the Potomac and contributed to the northern offensive against the Confederacy. At the end of the war, this excellent officer continued his military career as commander of various units of the U.S. Army before dying of pneumonia in 1872.

ANALYSIS OF THE BATTLE

DIRECTING THE WAR TO THE NORTH TO OBTAIN PEACE

Since the beginning of the war, the southerners had been struggling to achieve decisive results against the Unionists. Yet, it was vital that the battle was not bogged down after the numerous losses that had already reduced the ranks of the army. Therefore, in May 1863, after the Confederate victory at Chancellorsville, General Robert Edward Lee went to Richmond to convince President Jefferson Davis that it was imperative to wage a war on the territory of the Union. According to him, the Confederate could derive several advantages:

- This would primarily relieve the state of Virginia, where many fights took place;
- The Army of the Potomac would be forced to leave the strong positions it held and fight in conditions that were less favorable;
- The large northern cities (Baltimore, Philadelphia, Washington, New York, etc.) would thus be endangered;
- Winning a significant victory in the north of the territory would probably convince the European courts to diplomatically recognize the Confederate and help in its fight;
- Finally, a decisive battle would launch peace negotiations from a position of strength.

These arguments eventually convinced Jefferson Davis and Robert Edward Lee received the order, on 3 June, to put his plan into action. Starting from Fredericksburg, the army of Northern Virginia, which had between 75 000 and 80 000 men, went to the northern territory of Pennsylvania. This army, rebuilt after the victory at Chancellorsville, was composed of three corps and a powerful cavalry force. While James Longstreet directed the first corps and James Ewell Brown Stuart (1833-1864) led the cavalry, two new commanders were assigned to the 2nd and 3rd corps: Richard Stoddert Ewell (1817-1872) to the 2nd corps and Ambrose Powell Hill (1825-1865) to the 3rd.Robert Edward Lee's plan was as follows: hidden in the Shenandoah Valley, the widely spaced corps should move due north, crossing the Potomac River to enter Pennsylvania and eventually try to take the administrative capital of the region, Harrisburg.

Good to know

The southern army which penetrated into enemy territory had only very little food. It carried only ammunition and had to find food to meet their needs immediately. However, Robert Edward Lee gave his men strict orders to prevent looting. The northern historians themselves recognized the morality of the Confederate troops, in contrast to the devastation ordered by the northern leaders in the southern territory. Due to his nature as much as his upbringing, Robert Edward Lee refused to wage total war. In addition, he was always secretly hoping for reconciliation and therefore wished to put the odds on his side.

ERROR AND STRATEGIES

It was not until 8 June that the Union understood that the southern army used the valleys as the axis of penetration. Ignoring the significance of the enemy forces, the commander of the Army of the Potomac, Joseph Hooker, would directly attack its rear. However, President Abraham Lincoln forbade him from doing so because he did not want to leave the big cities without protection. Therefore, the strategy was to follow the enemy flank and to attack when the opportunity arose. Joseph Hooker, who had lost the confidence of many Unionist leaders after his defeat at Chancellorsville, thus went north, merely acting as a screen between the major cities in the Union and his opponents.

While the two armies moved towards the northern United States in June 1863, each of them knew exactly where the other was located. General Joseph Hooker, pressed by the president who wanted to destroy the Confederate Army, hesitated and failed to penetrate the intentions of Robert Edward Lee. The population of Pennsylvania, who saw the enemy approaching, was also beginning to panic. In fact, from 20-26 June, various spaced army corps under the commander of the Confederate crossed the Potomac. Although everything went as expected, Confederate General James Ewell Brown Stuart committed a serious mistake on 25 June: without obtaining the agreement of Robert Edward Lee, he undertook a raid with all his cavalry on the major Unionist cities in order to scare more people. However, by placing himself to the east of the Union army, he was cut off from the commander in chief and was unable to inform him at the decisive moment.

On 28 June, Robert Edward Lee learned from a spy that the army of Joseph Hooker was moving up through the north. Hoping that the Potomac army would be further south, he found that it was actually extremely close. Therefore, he decided to gather his armies around Gettysburg and then to continue north to take the Unionists on favorable ground where he could defeat them. That same day, Joseph Hooker was replaced by General George Gordon Meade, to the dismay of the latter. Given the refusal of the President to send additional reinforcements, Joseph Hooker had sent his resignation letter to Abraham Lincoln two days earlier, who, furious, had accepted it. George Gordon Meade took the decision to tread carefully north with his army of about 90 000 men, in order to prevent the Confederate army from penetrating further into Union territory. The planned marching route passed through the small town of Gettysburg.

30 JUNE-1 JULY 1863: THE MEETING IN GETTYSBURG

The two armies knew that the fighting was close, but they did not know where or when it would occur. The 3rd corps of Confederate General Ambrose Powell Hill, awaiting the rest of the army, was the closest to Gettysburg. Learning that there was a shoe factory in this city, he allowed the division of General Henry Heth (1825-1899) to go there because shoes were sorely lacking in the Confederate army. However, the southerners were overtaken by the Brigadier

General of the Unionist cavalry, John Buford, who had settled in the city in a defensive position. General Henry Heth
and General Ambrose Powell Hill, believing that they were
militias, decided to wait until the next day to seize the city,
without notifying General Robert Edward Lee.

Expecting the Confederate forces to appear, the small cavalry division of John Buford settled in a defensive position
west of Gettysburg, having understood the importance of
this city, to which no less than twelve roads led. In addition,
the city, located between several hills, offered a certain
advantage to Unionist defenders. Having warned George
Gordon Meade of the presence of the enemy, John Buford
hoped to soon receive his help, without which the heights
of Gettysburg would be taken by the commander of the
Confederate, which would be very difficult to dislodge.
At around 8:00am, two brigades of General Henry Heth
appeared before the horsemen of John Buford. These, with
better armament, managed to contain the attackers. As
they were beginning to take the upper hand, the Unionist
Army Corps of General John Fulton Reynolds (1820-1863)
came to the rescue. However, shortly after warning George
Gordon Meade that the enemy was making strong progress,
he was shot on the battlefield. The announcement of the
clashes in Gettysburg was spreading rapidly in both camps.

The Fall of Reynolds, painting by Alfred Waud, 1863.

Having repelled the threat from the West, the Unionists defenders now had to turn to the north, where new southern troops were arriving. General Robert Edward Lee, who had just reached the battlefield, noted that the sector was more favorable to the Unionists and decided not to engage in general combat. Now the situation was very volatile and the Union front had already collapsed north of the city. The Confederates continued to receive reinforcements into the afternoon, which arrived from the east and the north, forcing the Unionist troops to gradually retreat towards the south, where the heights of the city were located. At the same time, the General of the Union, Winfield Scott Hancock (1824-1886) arrived, commissioned by George Gordon Meade to take over command from the late John Fulton Reynolds and reorganize the troops. Robert Edward Lee, unaware that he faced only a part of the Union army, did not fully commit to the fight as not all of his forces were reunited. He thus left it to the discretion of Confederate

General Richard Stoddert Ewell to decide whether to attack the northern defenders who were cornered in the south of the city. Having already lost about 8 000 men since the morning, General Ewell decided not to try anything and preferred to recover his strength when night fell.

However, it appeared that, on the first day of the fighting, the Confederates missed a huge opportunity to destroy part of the Potomac army before facing the bulk of it.

2 JULY 1863: CONFEDERATE ERRORS

During the night, the northerners were taking advantage of the end of the fighting to dig trenches, in order to strengthen their positions on the heights of the city. In the morning, the gathering of the southern forces was almost complete. All that was missing was the division of George Edward Pickett, while the other side had not yet received its reinforcements. The Confederate commander Robert Edward Lee was determined to fight the enemy that had fortified its position in the hills south of Gettysburg, although his subordinate, General James Longstreet, disapproved. Indeed, the latter thought that the southerners were headed for disaster and it would be better to fight in a place that would be more favorable to them. Convinced that his choice was correct, Robert Edward Lee prepared his plan of attack, which included:

- The 1st corps of James Longstreet that was stealthily positioned to the southwest of the Union Army in order to take the flank and push it back;

- At the same time, a unit of the 3rd Corps and two divisions of the 2nd Corps conducted a diversionary attack on the center and right of the Unionist front, to prevent the sending of reinforcements to the left, where the main attack would take place. If the opportunity arose, this diversion could become a real attack.

It was up to General James Longstreet to launch the operation. However, he showed no willingness to obey orders and did not act until after 4:00pm. Meanwhile, the meeting of the Union army had been achieved and General George Gordon Meade had had time to disperse his army, which formed an arc extending from the east, then north through the west and southwest. When James Longstreet finally launched the assault, he did not attack the southwest in order to encircle the northerners, but the west, where the hills of the Round Tops and the rocks of the Devil's Den were located. On an extremely challenging terrain for both sides, close combat fighting took place that would be among the most terrible of the war. Moreover, the combatants were bypassed in the south by the 15th Confederate regiment of Alabama which went to Little Round Top hill. If the southerners managed to take it, they would be able to install their artillery and enfilade the Union frontline over its entire length. Spotting the danger, the Unionists sent the 20th Main regiment commanded by Colonel Joshua Lawrence Chamberlain (1828-1914). Along with his 386 men, he conducted bloody fights that would end with a bayonet charge that would later become famous, in order to save the left flank of the Union army, avoiding its defeat.

Meanwhile, at the center of the northern device, the 3rd Confederate corps managed to repel the troops of George Gorgon Meade. However, having received no specific orders and with little support, General Ambrose Powell Hill did not dare to push the offensive further and decided to retreat. Finally, on the right wing of the Unionist forces, two divisions of the 2nd corps of Richard Stoddert Ewell, which were supposed to attack at the same time as James Longstreet, were launched around 5:00pm, not having heard the cannon that signaled the start of the attack. They faced retrenchments and powerful artillery that crushed them when they reached the slopes.

At nightfall, the clashes came to an end. The offensive that intended to overthrow the Unionist Front had failed. This was partly due to the poor coordination of the three Confederate attacks, but also the promptness of the Unionists in sending reinforcements where they were nee-ded most. However, on the night of 2-3 July, Robert Edward Lee decided to continue fighting, while General James Longstreet once again wished to give up. For the first time, the southern army had to definitively destroy the Union Army, as the fate of the Confederacy depended on it.

In the northern camp, the generals held a council of war, where it was unanimously decided, despite the considerable losses, to remain in position and wait for the enemy attack once again. Therefore, George Gordon Meade used that night to strengthen the left wing of the device, as well as the center, which he expected to be the main target of the enemy offensive the following day.

3 JULY 1863: THE BURDEN OF GEORGE EDWARD PICKETT

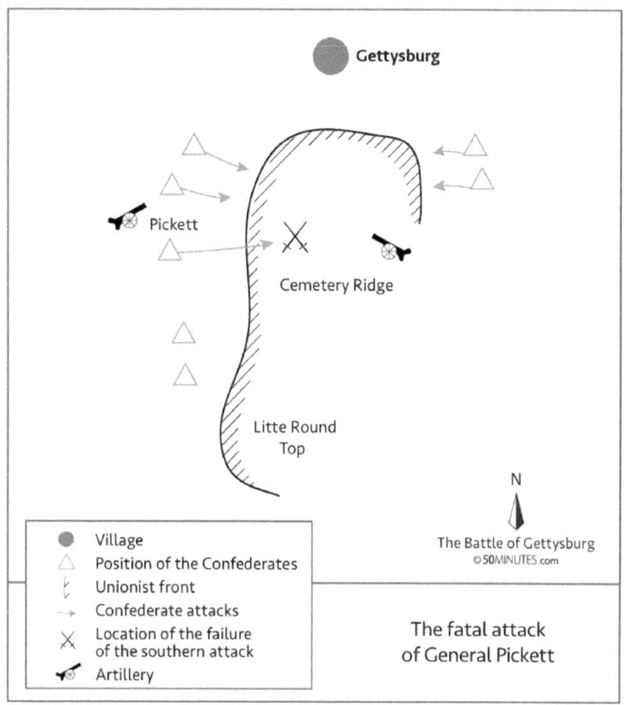

The fatal attack
of General Pickett

On 3 July, in the southern camp, the division of George Edward Pickett finally joined the 1st corps of James Longstreet. Moreover, James Ewell Brown Stuart finally managed to find the Confederate army, but his men were truly exhausted.

The battle plan for the day was as follows:

- Commanding almost all of the artillery of the Confederate Army (130-150 canons) to massively fire at the Unionist line of defense in order to weaken it before the real attack began;
- Launching the 2nd corps of Richard Stoddert Ewell once again to the right of the Unionist front in order to encourage the enemy to keep large forces on the wings and thin out the center, which would be the main target of the attack;
- Putting James Longstreet in charge of leading the division of George Edward Pickett and six brigades belonging to the corps of Ambrose Powell Hill in a frontal assault against the center of the northern front.

Hancock at Gettysburg by Thure de Thulstrup, 1887. Showing Pickett's Charge.

As expected, the battle began in the morning on the right of the Unionist front. However, this wing had been strengthened overnight and the fighting quickly became very intense. The fight lasted no less than seven hours, after which the Confederates eventually retreated. Meanwhile, the artillery of the Confederate Army was brought against the northern center and was put into action shortly after 1pm. The Unionists, who noticed the preparations for the attack, also positioned 80 canons to fight back.

Then, for almost two hours, the most formidable artillery duel that the United States had ever known took place. While the southerners' guns were perfectly adjusted, the gunners did however make the mistake of not concentrating their fire on the salient where the assault would be given. At 3pm, while the Confederate ammunition was exhausted, the 15 000 men led by George Edward Pickett raced to the heights where the center of the army of General George Gordon Meade was located. Waiting until they were within firing range, the Unionists gunners unleashed their guns, whose shells rained down on the southern ranks. The northern infantry in turn opened fire. The ranks of the Confederate general division were devastated, but still managed to reach the heights of Cemetery Ridge. Northern General Winfield Scott Hancock reacted immediately and ordered a violent counter-attack against the handful of assailants that were still alive. At 3:30pm, half of the men commanded by George Edward Pickett were lying on the battlefield, while the other half retreated towards the southern camp. The division had lost three quarters of its workforce and numerous officers. Confederate General

Robert Edward Lee, very distressed, admitted that the battle was lost and it was time to think about retreating.

The northern camp was relieved. George Gordon Meade knew that his opponent was defeated, but did not take the opportunity to attack, for which Abraham Lincoln would later blame him. He estimated that the losses were too numerous on both sides and particularly feared that Robert Edward Lee would set a trap if he launched a new offensive. On the night of 4-5 July, the threat to the major cities in the northern states was lifted.

REPERCUSSIONS OF THE BATTLE

The Battle of Gettysburg was undoubtedly the bloodiest of the Civil War, since there were no fewer than 20 000 casualties on both sides. The implications for the Confederate were primarily moral and political. Indeed, the southerners who fought with considerable effort could not overcome the Union Army. The hope of a victory and favorable peace negotiations with the north disappeared. However, the prestige of the Commander-in-Chief was not affected by this defeat. The southerners trusted him completely, but knew that they could not, for lack of resources, undertake a new offensive in Union territory. Henceforth, the initiative lay with the Union and the southerners would simply wage a defensive war. With the defeat at Gettysburg, they also lost hope of receiving any help from the European courts. The latter, observing that the war was taking a turn for the worst for the Confederacy, would not recognize it and would never come to its aid.

In the northern camp, enthusiasm initially reigned. But, this was short lived. Learning that Robert Edward Lee's army had not been destroyed, joy immediately disappeared. However, it should be noted that the victory of Gettysburg, combined with that of General Ulysses S. Grant (1822-1885) in Vicksburg on 4 July 1863, galvanized the leaders of the Union and led them to resume the offensive. Thus, from the second half of 1863 until the surrender of the Confederate in 1865, the Union would constantly lead the offensive against an enemy that had only a defensive option.

Finally, four months after the battle of Gettysburg, on 13 November 1863, President Abraham Lincoln visited the battlefield and delivered a speech during the inauguration of the cemetery of Gettysburg, where the victims of both sides lay. In this moving speech, which became very famous, the 16th President of the United States made a brief tribute to the victims of both sides and called on the founding values of the American nation, namely equality and freedom.

President Abraham Lincoln's speech during the inauguration of the cemetery of Gettysburg.

SUMMARY

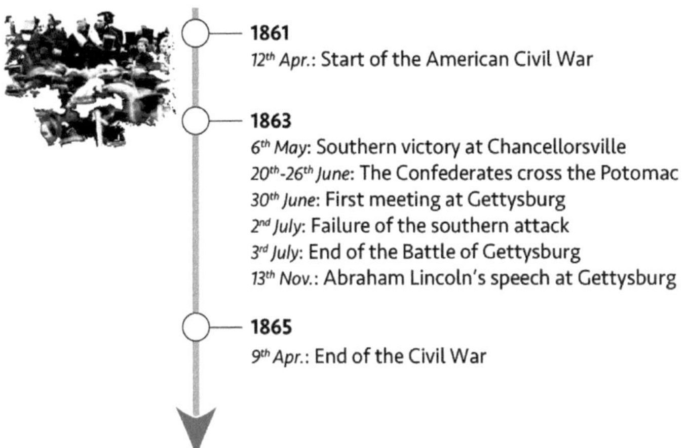

1861
12th Apr.: Start of the American Civil War

1863
6th May: Southern victory at Chancellorsville
20th-26th June: The Confederates cross the Potomac
30th June: First meeting at Gettysburg
2nd July: Failure of the southern attack
3rd July: End of the Battle of Gettysburg
13th Nov.: Abraham Lincoln's speech at Gettysburg

1865
9th Apr.: End of the Civil War

- Since the 1850s, the American nation was experiencing a deep crisis that saw many states oppose each other over slavery. While the northern states wished to abolish slavery, the southern states wanted to maintain it to save their economies.
- Tensions between the two sides culminated when Abraham Lincoln was elected president on 4th March 1861. Refusing to be led by an abolitionist, the southern states decided to secede and elect an interim president, Jefferson Davis.
- Therefore, Abraham Lincoln, who refused separation, appeared ready to use force to bring the south into the Union. The Civil War broke out on 12 April 1861.
- In June 1863, General Robert Edward Lee convinced Jefferson Davis to conduct the war in the Union territory

in order to decide the fate of the war.
- On 8 June, the Union army set off in pursuit of its opponent and waited for the right moment to attack.
- On 28 June, while the confrontation was approaching, Joseph Hooker resigned and was replaced by George Gordon Meade.
- Two days later, the first meeting between the two camps took place at Gettysburg.
- On 1 July, the vanguards of each army clashed, but the Confederates did not dare to launch a major offensive as the bulk of their forces had not yet gathered.
- On 2 July, following a heroic resistance from the Unionist troops and through a lack of coordination, the Confederates were unable to take over their opponent.
- In the evening, while General Robert Edward Lee decided to lead the final assault the next day, the Unionist staff chose to resist. On 3 July, after a major battle, the Confederate artillery units attacked the center of the enemy device.
- The Unionists managed to resist and won the violent battle.
- Recognizing the importance of the losses and the defeat, Robert Edward Lee accepted defeat and chose to retreat.

We want to hear from you!
Leave a comment on your online library
and share your favourite books on social media!

FIND OUT MORE

BIBLIOGRAPHY

- Belperron, P. (1947) *La guerre de Sécession (1861-1865). Ses causes et ses suites*. Paris: Plon.
- Bowman, J. S. (1994) Lee, Robert Edward. In *Who Was Who in the Civil War*. New York: Crescent Books.
- Bowman, J. S. (1994) Meade, George Gordon. In *Who Was Who in the Civil War*. New York: Crescent Books.
- Bowman, J. S. (1994) Pickett, George Edward. In *Who Was Who in the Civil War*. New York: Crescent Books.
- Catton, B. (1985) *The Civil War*. New York: American Heritage Publishing Co.
- Duncan, A.C. (2007) La guerre de Sécession. *Revue d'histoire du XIXe siècle*, Volume 35.
- Keegan, J. (2010) *The American Civil War*. London: Vintage.
- Kennett, L. (1997) *Gettysburg. 1863. Le tournant de la guerre de Sécession*. Paris: Économica.
- Portes, J. (2010) *Histoire des États-Unis. De 1776 à nos jours*. Paris: Armand Colin.
- Venner, D. (1995) *Gettysburg*. Monaco: Éditions du Rocher.
- Vallaud D. (1995) Gettysburg. In *Dictionnaire historique*. Paris: Fayard.
- Vallaud D. (1995) Lee, Robert Edward. In *Dictionnaire historique*. Paris: Fayard.

ADDITIONAL SOURCES

- Freeman, H. (2016) *Battle of Gettsyburg: A History from Beginning to End*. CreateSpace Independent Publishing Platform.
- Reardon, C. (1997) *Pickett's Charge in History and Memory*. Chapel Hill: University of North Carolina Press.
- Sauers, R. (2003) *Gettysburg: the Meade-Sickles Controversy*. Washington DC: Brassey's.
- Salmon, J. (2007) *Historic Photos of Gettysburg*. Nashville: Turner Publishing Company.
- Sears, S.W. (2008) *Gettysburg*. Boston: Mariner Books.
- Symonds C. (2001) *American Heritage. History of the Battle of Gettysburg*. New York: Harper Collins.

ICONOGRAPHIC SOURCES

- Portrait of Robert Edward Lee by Julian Vannerson. © *The Library of Congress Prints & Photographs*.
- Portrait of George Edward Pickett. Royalty-free reproduction picture.
- Portrait of George Gordon Meade by Matthew Brady. © *The Library of Congress Prints & Photographs*.
- *The Fall of Reynolds* by Alfred Waud, 1863. Royalty-free reproduction picture.
- *Hancock at Gettysburg* by Thure de Thulstrup, 1887. Royalty-free reproduction picture.
- Lincoln's speech during the inauguration of Gettysburg cemetery. © *The Library of Congress Prints & Photographs*.

FILMS

- *Gettysburg*. (1993) [Film]. Ronald Maxwell. Dir. USA: Turner Pictures/TriStar Television.

NOVELS

- Shaara, M. (2013) *The Killer Angels*. Edinburgh: Birlinn Limited.

OTHER

- *Battle of Gettysburg*, painting by Thure de Thulstrup (American artist, 1848-1930).

MUSEUMS AND COMMEMORATIVE BUILDINGS

- Gettysburg National Military Park, Pennsylvania (United States).

www.50minutes.com

Ebook EAN: 9782806273222

Paperback EAN: 9782806273239

Legal Deposit: D/2015/12603/642

Cover: © Primento

Digital conception by Primento, the digital partner of publishers.